Diet recommendations for TCM - Heart - Fire

Please check these recommendations always with a TCM nutrition consultant, therapist, doctor or dietician. The recipes and the list of ingredients are supporting also the conventional medical therapy. The calorie disclosures of fresh ingredients (fruit and vegetables) vary according to quality and time of harvest. The contents were checked by a dietician and a nutrition consultant for the Traditional Chinese Medicine (TCM).

Author:
©2017 Josef Miligui
www.ebns.at

AF220173

Source:
The lists are created from the EBNS database for nutritional counseling. The database is used by dietitians, therapists and doctors for advising the patient / client.

Literature:
The specialist literature and the training documents of the German and Austrian dietary and traditional Chinese medicine serve as a knowledge base. We have used the documents as a basis of knowledge, adapted it to our experience and completed them
http://di-book.com

Title Photo:
©2008 Erika Weixlbaumer

Production and publishing:
BoD – Books on Demand, Norderstedt
ISBN: 9783752862232

Diet recommendations for TCM - Heart - Fire

1   Treatment strategy

Cool heat and dissipate. Calm the mind, nourish the heart and kidneys
Yin, cool. - NO, warm little to NO, everything else YES.

2   Avoid

Bitter, drying, hot spices, very salty, grilled, fried, toasted, Yogitee,
cocoa, chocolate, hectic, stress, screen work, go to bed late.

3 Breakfast

4 Snack

5 Lunch

6 Afternoon

7 Dinner

8 Any time

9   Recipes

(recommendable) = You can use more.
(little) = You should use less than specified or omit.

9.1   8 treasures of rice

Strengthens kidney and bladder, builds up Qi, strengthens the spleen, repels moisture, reduces internal heat, prevents cancer, builds heart, calms nerves.
Cooking time approx. 1 hour
Calories p. portion: 212
4 portions

Quantity of ingredients
Lily bulbs 1 table spoon / 5g. (recommended)................................... *
Longane 1 table spoon / 5g. (little).. *
King Solomon's-seal 1 table spoon / 5g. (recommended)................. *
Yam root, yam root tuber 1 table spoon / 5g. (recommended)........... *
Coix (seeds) YiYi Ren 1 table spoon / 5g. (yes)............................... *
Rice wild (nature rice) 1 1/2 cups / 240g. (little)..........................metal
Water 8-10 cups / 800g. (yes) .... earth

Cooking instructions:
Each one 1 tbsp: Bai He, Longan, Yu Zhu, Da Zao, Shan Yao, Lian Mi, Yi Yi Ren, Qian Shi
Add hot water and soak for about 30 minutes. Then add 1 - 2 cups of rice (normal) and simmer for 1/2 to 1 hour until the rice is very soft. Or: Cook for about 3 hours with the herbs a congee. Then the herbs do not have to be soaked.

9.2   Adzuki Bean and Rice Soup

Reduces moisture, directs down, reduces gastrointestinal heat, builds up essence, strengthens muscles after heat illness, builds up body fluids.
Cooking time approx. 2 hours
Calories p. portion: 199
1 portions

Quantity of ingredients
Adzuki beans 8 table spoons / 40g. (yes) .... water
Rice round grain 2 table spoons / 20g. (little) .... metal
Water 1 1/2 cups / 200g. (yes) .... earth
Honey 1 table spoon / 8g. (yes) .... earth

Cooking instructions:
Boil soaked adzuki beans and round grain rice in a ratio of 4: 1 in water until a thin pulp has formed. Sweet as needed; possibly puree.

Effect: This recipe strengthens kidney, spleen and stomach and is particularly suitable for mothers with too little milk flow.

9.3   Apple sauce with raisins

Nourishes fluids, reduces stomach heat, strengthens spleen, harmonizes stomach, moisturizes, relaxes, builds up Qi.
Cooking time approx. 25 min
Calories p. portion: 74
10 portions
Allergens: O

Quantity of ingredients
Apple (sweet) 2,2 lbs / 1000g. (yes) .... earth
Water 1/2 cup / 100g. (yes) .... earth
Raisins 1/8 lbs - 2oz / 50g. (little) .... earth

Cooking instructions:
Wash, peel and quarter the apples and remove the core. Put the apples with the water in a pot. Wash the raisins with hot water and add them. Cook at low heat for about 10 minutes, then allow to cool. For children up to 10 months, mash in the blender finely. For the larger ones, crush with the potato steamer. Fill and seal in a freezer or empty yoghurt jug. Close the yoghurt jug. Freeze in the shock freezer.
If necessary, thaw at room temperature for about 6 hours. (Lasting about 4 months).
The fruit mousse is intended as dessert or intermediate meal. It has an anti-digestive effect. In case of diarrhea give better banana.

9.4 Apricot and cranberry ice cream

Moisturizes, relaxes, builds up Qi, preserves the fluids.
Cooking time approx. 5 min
Calories p. portion: 106
2 portions

Quantity of ingredients
Apricots 3/4 lbs / 350g. (little) .... earth
Water 1/4 cup / 50g. (yes) .... earth
Cranberry 2 table spoons / 45g. (yes)... wood

Cooking instructions:
Mix the apricot juice with the cranberry syrup. Fill the juice into little
molds, place in the freezer and let it freeze in about 3 hours.

9.5 Avocado with lemon

Nourishes Yin from liver, lung and colon, moisturizes, distributes, cools
heat, preserves fluids, contracts.
Cooking time approx. 5 min
Calories p. portion: 289
1 portions

Quantity of ingredients
Avocado 1/2 piece / 120g. (recommended) .. .. earth
Lemon juice 1/2 piece / 10g. (yes)............... .... wood
Salt 1 pinch / 1g. (recommended)................ ....water

Cooking instructions:
Halve the avocado, remove the core, add the lemon juice, salt a little
and eat with a spoon.

9.6 Barley mash with plums

Forces spleen, cools bladder, diuretic, moisturizes intestines, relaxes,
builds up Qi, spreads, strengthens blood and fluids, regulates Qi, cools
liver fire, produces humors, strengthens Qi and Kidney Jing,
moisturizes, relaxes, builds up Qi, spreads.
Cooking time approx. 25 min
Calories p. portion: 107
5 portions
Allergens: AG

Quantity of ingredients

Water 10 cups / 1200g. (yes)... earth
Barley 1 cup / 120g. (recommended)... earth
Plum 1 cup / 120g. (yes) ....wood
Butter organic 2 teaspoons / 6g. (yes) .... earth
Sugar cane sugar 1/2 teaspoon / 2g. (yes) .... earth

Cooking instructions:
Grind coarse the barley and roast it dry. Add hot water, add ginger and cardamom and let it swell to a pulp in low heat. Core the plums and boil for 10 minutes with a little water. At the end, add the stewed plums, a little butter and sweetener.

Variant: If you want to go fast, you can use barley flakes instead of shot.

9.7   Basic recipe for a beef broth (clear)

Strengthens Qi and Yang, is very warming.
Cooking time approx. 4-8 hours
Calories p. portion: 114
10 portions
Allergens: O

Quantity of ingredients

Beef soup meat 1,1 lbs / 500g. .... earth
Beef meatbones 5/8 oz / 200g. .... earth
Vinegar (Red wine vinegar) 1 dash / 3g. ....wood
Juniper berry 8 pieces / 6g. .... fire
Rosemary 1 pinch / 1g. .... fire
Carrot 3 pieces / 210g. .... earth
Parsnip 2 pieces / 300g. .... fire
Leek 1 piece / 200g. ....metal
Ginger fresh 1/2 teaspoon / 5g. ....metal
Lovage 1 stem / 15g. ....metal
Clove 2 pieces / 2g. ....metal
Pimento 6 pieces / 12g. ....metal
Anise (Common Fennel) 2 pieces / 1g. .... earth
Salt 1 teaspoon / 5g. ....water
Water 3,3 lbs / 1300g. .... earth

Cooking instructions:

Heat water, a dash of red wine vinegar, some juniper berries, a little rosemary, bones and meat till it boils; add carrot, parsnip, leek, ginger, lovage, clove, allspice, star anise and a little salt; simmer for 4-8 hours then strain.
Refrigerate for later use.

9.8 Basic recipe for a chicken broth worming

Strengthens Qi and blood, is very warm.
Cooking time approx. 2-3 hours
Calories p. portion: 90
9 portions
Allergens: L

Quantity of ingredients

Chicken meat 1/2 piece / 600g. ....wood
Carrot 2 pieces / 150g. .... earth
Leek 1 stick / 45g. ....metal
Celery root 1 piece / 500g. .... earth
Ginger fresh 2 slices / 2g. ....metal
Fenugreek (Trigonella foenum-graecum) 1 teaspoon / 2g. ....*
Juniper berry 1 teaspoon / 3g. .... fire
Bay leaf 3 pieces / 2g. .... *
Water 4 cup / 900g. .... earth

Cooking instructions:

Remove chicken parts from fat. Place chicken pieces in a saucepan with hot water and heat till it boils briefly, skimming any resulting foam. Add coarsely chopped vegetables and all spices and cook over medium heat for 2 to 3 hours. Strain the finished soup. Throw away vegetables and bones.
Tip: If you want to use the meat as a soup insert, take out after 45 minutes and return only the bones in the soup.
Refrigerate for later use.

9.9 Basic recipe for a duck broth

Forces Qi, strengthens blood and fluids, nourishes Yin, forces stomach, cools heat, strengthens spleen and liver.
Cooking time approx. 2-3 hours
Calories p. portion: 61
6 portions
Allergens: L

Quantity of ingredients
Duck (heart) 5/8 oz / 200g. .... wood
Water 2 cup / 450g. .... earth
Duck (slaughtered) 1/4 lbs - 4oz / 100g. .... wood
Carrot 2 pieces / 100g. .... earth
Celery root 1/2 piece / 600g. .... earth

Cooking instructions:
Cook duck pieces with vegetables for 2-3 hours. Sift broth through a fine sieve and refrigerate for later use.
The innards can be reused: You cut them finely and leaves them for a few minutes with fresh vegetables in the broth draw. Sprinkle with parsley before serving.

9.10 Basic recipe for a fish broth

Strengthens kidney Qi and Yin, strengthens blood and fluids, promotes urination.
Cooking time approx. 40 min
Calories p. portion: 128
5 portions
Allergens: DLO

Quantity of ingredients
Fish pieces mixed (fresh water) 3/4 lbs / 300g. .... water
Celery root 1/4 lbs - 4oz / 120g. .... earth
Leek 2 inches / 10g. .... metal
Carrot 2 pieces / 150g. .... earth
White wine 1/2 cup / 125g. .... wood
Lemon 1/2 piece / 50g. .... wood
Bay leaf 2 leaves / 2g. .... *
Peppercorns 3 pieces / 2g. .... metal
Olive oil 1 table spoon / 10g. .... earth
Water 2 cup / 450g. .... earth

Cooking instructions:
Fry celery, chopped carrots and leeks in olive oil, add bay leaf and peppercorns, add pieces of fish and sauté briefly. Add water, add little white wine or lemon. Simmer gently for 30 minutes. Skim off the resulting foam several times. In the end, sift the ingredients through a cloth.
Refrigerate for later use.

9.11 Basic recipe for a reissue soup (Congee)

Warms the stomach and spleen, harmonizes the intestine, forces Qi, reduces moisture.
Cooking time approx. 2-4 hours
Calories p. portion: 140
3 portions
Allergens:

Quantity of ingredients
Rice variety any 1 cup / 120g.   ....metal
Water 6 cups / 700g.   .... earth

Cooking instructions:
Cook rice and water in a ratio of about 1: 6. The amount of water determines the thickness of the mash (matter of taste).
Put the rice in a saucepan with a heavy lid. It is important to simmer the rice after a short boil on the slightest flame, otherwise it burns.
Boil the rice for 2-4 hours. The longer he cooks, the more he strengthens.
If you want to eat the dish for breakfast, you can put the rice on just before bedtime.
To be on the safe side, you should first check the behavior of your pot and cooker under observation for a similar amount of time, so that nothing burns.
Refrigerate for later use.

9.12 Basic recipe for a vegetable soup, nutritious

Strengthens spleen and lung, regulates Qi flow, builds up Qi, dries out, passes downwardly, strengthens stomach Qi.
Cooking time approx. 2-3 hours
Calories p. portion: 48
5 portions
Allergens: L

Quantity of ingredients

Olive oil 1 table spoon / 4g. .... earth
Onion white 1 piece / 60g. ....metal
Carrot 3 pieces / 200g. .... earth
Parsnip 3/8 lbs - 6oz / 150g. .... fire
Celery root 1 cup / 100g. .... earth
Ginger fresh 1/2 teaspoon / 2g. ....metal
Lemon 1/2 piece / 25g. ....wood
Juniper berry 6 pieces / 6g. .... fire
Thyme dried 1 pinch / 1g. ....metal
Lovage 1 table spoon / 3g. ....metal
Bay leaf 2 leaves / 1g. .... *
Salt 1 pinch / 1g. ....water
Water 3 cups / 650g. .... earth

Cooking instructions:
Cut the vegetables into cubes.
Heat oil in hot pot, fry shortly onions and vegetables.
Add cold water, then add ginger, bay leaf and lemon juice.
Season with juniper, thyme and lovage. Cover for 2 - 3 hours on a low heat and simmer.
The used vegetables should be thrown away.
The basic recipe serves as a soup base and to refine vegetables, legumes or cereals.
If you want to eat vegetable soup immediately, add the desired vegetables half an hour before. Refrigerate for later use.

9.13 Black root with yogurt

Nourishes Yin, relaxes, builds up Qi, moisturises dryness, preserves the fluids.
Cooking time approx. 20 min
Calories p. portion: 424
2 portions
Allergens: AG

Quantity of ingredients

Salsify 1 lbs / 400g. (yes) .... earth
Yogurt (natural, 1.5% fat) 4 table spoons / 80g. (recommended)... fire
Herbs various 1 table spoon / 8g. (recommended)............................ *
Salt 1 pinch / 1g. (recommended)...water
Herbs various 2 table spoons / 6g. (recommended).......................... *
Multi-grain bread (gray bread) 6 slices / 120g. (recommended).. wood

Cooking instructions:
Peel the salsify and simmer in salted water until tender. Pour away the water, cool the salsify and cut it to size. Cover with yoghurt and sprinkle with fresh herbs. Serve with the bread.
You can also use the salsify from the conserve.

9.14 Chicken soup with angelica root and buckthorn fruit

Strengthens spleen and nourishes the blood and Yin of the liver, forces Qi and blood, is very warming.
Cooking time approx. 1 1/2 hours
Calories p. portion: 77
3 portions
Allergens: LO

Quantity of ingredients
Basic recipe for a chicken soup 2 cup / 500g. (recommended)..........*
Angelica root 1/8 oz / 5g. (recommended) ....*
Bocksdorn fruits, goji berry dried 1/8 lbs - 2oz / 50g. ....wood

Cooking instructions:
When you cook chicken broth according to basic recipes add angelica root and Bocksdorn fruits in the last 40 minutes.
Ingestion: Drink 2-3 cups of broth daily.

9.15 Compote from rhubarb

Cools heat, preserves the fluids, contracts, strengthens middle heater, moisturizes.
Cooking time approx. 15 min
Calories p. portion: 48
1 portions

Quantity of ingredients
Rhubarb 1/4 lbs - 4oz / 100g. (yes).... ....wood
Water 1 cup / 120g. (yes)... earth
Honey 1 table spoon / 10g. (yes)... earth

Cooking instructions:
Wash rhubarb and cut small. Boil in the water. Allow to cool a little and add the honey.

9.16 Cooling rice dish with grapefruit

Lowers lung Qi, nourishes fluids, dissolves mucus, dries out, passes downwardly, warms the stomach and spleen, harmonizes the intestine, forces Qi, reduces moisture, strengthens Qi and Kidney Jing, moisturizes, relaxes, builds up Qi, spreads.
Cooking time approx. 20 min
Calories p. portion: 234
4 portions
Allergens: GHO

Quantity of ingredients

Rice round grain 1 cup / 120g. (little) ....metal
Water 5 cups / 600g. (yes) .... earth
Hazelnuts 2 table spoons / 20g. (yes).. earth
Raisins 2 table spoons / 20g. (little) .... earth
Agave nectar 1 table spoon / 10g. (recommended)...........................*
Salt 1 pinch / 0,2g. (recommended)...water
Almond puree 1 table spoon / 10g. (little)................................ earth
Grapefruit (Pomelo) 1 piece / 200g. (yes) .... fire
Butter organic 2 teaspoons / 20g. (yes) .... earth

Cooking instructions:

Preparation on the eve: Pour round grain rice into cold water and cook. Soak chopped hazelnuts and raisins in some hot water overnight.

In the morning: Stir in a little hot water some agave syrup; add the rice and heat; add a small pinch of salt, almond paste, chopped grapefruit, the soaked chopped hazelnuts and raisins and mix; Serve with a small piece of butter.

9.17 Cream cheese substitute

Cools heat, keeps fluids, builds up blood and Yin.
Cooking time approx. 20 min
Calories p. portion: 526
2 portions
Allergens: AE

Quantity of ingredients

Soybean milk 4 cup / 300g. (yes)... earth
Lemon 1 piece / 50g. (recommended) .... wood
Herbs various 2 table spoons / 6g. (recommended)..........................*
Whole grain bread 6 slices / 300g. (recommended) .... wood

Cooking instructions:
Heat the soy milk in a saucepan till it boils, stirring occasionally (gets burn easily!), Then allow to cool.
Squeeze out the lemon and stir gently under the cooled soy milk (approx. 80°C/176°F), let it approx. 20 min. rest or clot.
Pour chopped soy milk through a strainer lined with a dishcloth, allow liquid to drain and then squeeze out remaining liquid with the dishcloth.
Refine to taste with fresh herbs.
Serve with wholemeal bread.

9.18 Creamy potatoes with cauliflower

Forces Qi, forces spleen, relieves inflammation, moisturizes, relaxes, builds up Qi, spreads, nourishes lung Yin, produces humors, cools inner heat, strengthens Qi and kidney Jing, harmon zes liver and spleen, forces eyesight.
Cooking time approx. 30 min
Calories p. portion: 332
1 portions
Allergens: CG

Quantity of ingredients
Potato 3/8 lbs - 6oz / 150g. (yes)... earth
Cauliflower 1/8 lbs - 2oz / 50g. (yes)... earth
Cow's milk (whole milk 3.5% fat) 2 table spoons / 30g. (yes).............*
Cream, sweet 30% 1 table spoon / 1Cg. (yes)...................................*
Butter organic 1 teaspoon / 10g. (yes)....................................... earth
Parsley 1 teaspoon / 3g. (little).. wood
Chicken yolk 1 piece / 25g. (recommended) .... earth

Cooking instructions:
Wash the potatoes under running water, thoroughly wash the cauliflower in stagnant water.
Divide the cauliflower florets into small buds, cut the stems into pieces about 1 cm in size.
Peel the potatoes and cut into 2 cm cubes.
Heat the milk with the cream in a saucepan, add the potatoes and the cauliflower. Cook on low heat for about 15 minutes.
Put the vegetables in a plate, add the butter, the chopped parsley and the egg yolk and lightly knead and mix everything with a fork.

9.19 Curdcheesedumplings on strawberry pulp

Preserves the fluids, contracts, moisturizes the lungs, nourishes liver-blood, relaxes.
Cooking time approx. 30 min
Calories p. portion: 553
5 portions
Allergens: ACG

Quantity of ingredients
Curd cheese 20% 1,1 lbs / 500g. (yes)... *
Spelled semolina 3/8 lbs - 6oz / 150g. (yes)............................... wood
Butter organic 1/8 lbs - 2oz / 40g. (yes) .... earth
Chicken egg 2 pieces / 120g. (yes).. earth
Sugar - icing sugar 2 table spoons / 20g. (recommended) .... earth
Salt 1 pinch / 1g. (recommended)... water
Breadcrumbs 2 table spoons / 25g. (recommended)................... wood
Butter organic 1/4 lbs - 4oz / 100g. (yes) .... earth
Strawberries 1,1 lbs / 500g. (yes) .... wood
Sugar - icing sugar 2 table spoons / 25g. (recommended) .... earth

Cooking instructions:
Curdcheese, grit, butter, eggs, powdered sugar and salt to a smooth dough. Keep the dough 15 mins in the refrigerator to settle down. Then shape small dumplings with a diameter of approx 4cm and boil them for about 10 minutes in slightly boiling salt water. Heat butter in a pan and roast the breadcrumbs golden brown. Roll the dumplings carefully into the crumbs.
Serve the dumplings with the strawberry.

9.20 Fennel-Rice Soup

Regulates Qi, warms the inside, lowers cold, forces stomach, relieves constipation, forces Yang, dissolves mucus, reduces wind, spreads, strengthens Qi and kidney Jing, builds up Qi.
Cooking time approx. 15-20 min
Calories p. portion: 156
2 portions
Allergens: EG

Quantity of ingredients
Basic recipe for a rice soup (Congee) 1 cup / 300g. (recommended) *
Fennel 1/2 piece / 150g. (recommended) .... earth
Butter organic 1 table spoon / 15g. (yes) .... earth
Soy sauce 1 dash / 3g. (yes) ....water

Cooking instructions:
Cook the fennel softly in the rice soup according to the basic recipe.
Before serving, add a piece of butter and some soy sauce.

9.21 Grated apple

Preserves the fluids, contracts.
Cooking time approx. 10 min
Calories p. portion: 120
1 portions

Quantity of ingredients
Apple (sour) 1 piece / 200g. (yes)..wood

Cooking instructions:
Peel apple and grate as fine as possible. Leave for at least 5 minutes
until it turns brown.

9.22 Kudzu soup in the morning

Moisturizes, relaxes, builds up Qi, spreads, forces stomach, harmonizes
middle, reduces internal heat, detoxifies, softens, passes downwardly.
Cooking time approx. 5 min
Calories p. portion: 12
1 portions
Allergens: E

Quantity of ingredients
Water 1 cup / 250g. (yes) .... earth
Soy sauce 1 dash / 2g. (yes) ....water
Umeboshi paste 1 knife tip / 2g. (recommended) ....water

Cooking instructions:
Mix kudzu with cold water and heat till it boils while stirring. Once it is
glassy, remove from heat and let cool. Season with Tamari and
Umeboshipaste or crushed umeboshi plums
There is always the possibility to support your stomach and intestines
with this recipe, taken before the right breakfast.

A morning cure for stomach and mucous membranes. Fix the base balance.

9.23 Melanzani with olive oil and turmeric

Cools and moves blood, reduces external and internal wind, reduces internal heat, nourishes liver-Yin, cools heat, produces humors, moisturizes, relaxes, builds up Qi, spreads.
Cooking time approx. 30 min
Calories p. portion: 432
2 portions
Allergens: A

Quantity of ingredients
Aubergine 2 pieces / 300g. (yes) .... earth
Olive oil 4 table spoons / 60g. (recommended) .... earth
Tomato 4 pieces / 200g. (recommended) .... wood
Turmeric (yellow root) 1/2 teaspoon / 1g. (recommended) .... *
Ground 1 pinch / 1g. (recommended) .... earth
Salt 1 pinch / 1g. (recommended) .... water
White bread (wheat bread) 4 slices / 80g. (recommended) .... wood

Cooking instructions:
Cut the melanzani into slices and spread them with the tomatoes on a baking tray. Sprinkle with olive oil and then with turmeric, caraway and salt. Bake them in the tube 20 min.
Serve with the white bread.

9.24 Potato pancakes

Forces Qi, forces spleen, relieves inflammation, moisturizes, relaxes, builds up Qi, spreads, forces blood, Yin and Jing, nourishes Yin, Moisturizes in case of internal dryness, forces blood, forces spleen, calms nerves and stomach.
Cooking time approx. 15 min
Calories p. portion: 893
1 portions
Allergens: ACG

Quantity of ingredients
Potato (mealy) 5/8 lbs - 8oz / 250g. (recommended).................. earth
Wheat flour 1/2 oz / 10g. (yes)..wood
Chicken egg 1 piece / 35g. (yes) .... earth
Rapeseed oil 2 table spoons / 20g. (yes).................................. earth
Salt 1 pinch / 1g. (recommended)...water
Cream sour 20% 1/8 lbs - 2oz / 50g. (recommended).......................*
Salt 1 pinch / 1g. (recommended)...water
Herbs various 1 table spoon / 10g. (recommended).........................*

Cooking instructions:
Grater the peeled potatoes finely, add the remaining ingredients, mix well and salt. Heat the oil and add small flat cakes to the pan with the spoon. Roast the potato pancakes on both sides crispy golden brown. Place them on the plate with sour cream, salt and sprinkle with herbs.

9.25 Potatoes with wild garlic-curd cheese

Forces Qi, forces spleen, relieves inflammation, nourishes blood and Yi, forces Zang-organs, forces stomach and intestines, harmonizes Qi, Relieves alcohol poisoning, moisturizes lungs, gets Qi moving.
Cooking time approx. 20 min
Calories p. portion: 254
2 portions
Allergens: G

Quantity of ingredients
Potato 3/4 lbs / 300g. (yes).. earth
Salt 1 pinch / 0,1g. (recommended)..water
Wild garlic (garlic spinach) 2 handful / 30g. (recommended) ......metal
Curd cheese 20% 5/8 lbs - 8oz / 250g. (yes) ....*
Yogurt (natural, 1.5% fat) 2 table spoons / 20g. (recommended)... fire
Salt 1 pinch / 1g. (recommended)...water

Cooking instructions:
Cook potatoes in salted water and peel.
Wash he wild garlic leaves and carefully dried and cut into fine strips. Mix the cottage cheese, yogurt and salt and mix in the chopped wild garlic pieces. Serve with the potatoes.
In the season in which no wild garlic grows the wild garlic pesto can be used.

9.26 Reissue soup with duck

Nourishes Yin, warms the stomach and spleen, harmonizes the intestine, forces Qi, reduces moisture,nourishes blood and liver, harmonizes liver and spleen, moisturizes, relaxes, builds up Qi, spreads.
Cooking time approx. 1 1/2 hours
Calories p. portion: 161
6 portions
Allergens: EG

Quantity of ingredients
Rice round grain 1 cup / 100g. (little) ....metal
Water 8 cups / 900g. (yes) .... earth
Duck (slaughtered) 5/8 lbs - 8oz / 250g. (recommended)...........wood
Shiitake, dried 4-6 pieces / 5g. (yes).. earth
Parsley 2 table spoons / 12g. (little)...wood
Butter organic 1 teaspoon / 3g. (yes)... earth
Soy sauce 1 dash / 2g. (yes) ....water

Cooking instructions:
Soak shiitake mushrooms. Prepare rice soup according to the basic recipe. Add duck meat and shiitake mushrooms for the last 30 minutes. Add oyster mushrooms, parsley and a little butter at the very end. Season with soy sauce.

Variant: Add soaked and cooked adzuki beans. They enhance the diuretic effect.

9.27 Rice congee with dried fruit

Warms the stomach and spleen, harmonizes the intestine, forces Qi, reduces moisture, nourishes blood and Yi, harmonizes lungs Qi, strengthens Qi and kidney Jing, moisturizes, relaxes, builds up Qi, spreads.
Cooking time approx. 10 min
Calories p. portion: 210
2 portions
Allergens: GO

Quantity of ingredients

Basic recipe for a rice soup (Congee) 4 cups / 500g. (recommended)*
Butter organic 1/2 teaspoon / 5g. (yes) .... earth
Apricot dried 6 table spoons / 50g. (recommended) .... earth
Water 1/2 cup / 50g. (yes) .... earth
Maple syrup 1 dash / 3g. (yes) .... earth

Cooking instructions:

Cook rice congee according to basic recipe.

Melt a small amount of butter over a low heat and briefly fry small dried fruit with 1/2 cup of water. Add the amount of rice porridge desired for the meal and heat. Serve hot and sweeten with maple syrup if necessary.
Variant: In addition fresh fruit with braise.

9.28 Rice with parsnips

Regulates Qi, dries out, passes downwardly, warms the stomach and spleen, harmonizes the intestine, forces Qi, reduces moisture.
moisturizes, relaxes, builds up Qi, spreads. distributes mucus, activates Wei Qi, forces Qi.
Cooking time approx. 45 min
Calories p. portion: 206
3 portions

Quantity of ingredients

Rice variety any 1 cup / 120g. (little) .... metal
Water 1 1/2 cups / 200g. (yes) .... earth
Salt 1 pinch / 1g. (recommended) .... water
Parsnip 3-4 pieces / 450g. (yes) .... fire
Olive oil 1 table spoon / 10g. (recommended) .... earth
Sage 1 teaspoon / 3g. (recommended) .... fire

Cooking instructions:

Peel the parsnips and cut into slices. Fry for a short time in oil. Add the rice and fry again for a short time. Add the water and cook it at least 30 min. Sprinkle with fresh chopped sage.

9.29 Rice with stewed vegetables

Dissipates heat and moisture.
Cooking time approx. 20 min
Calories p. portion: 166
2 portions
Allergens: L

Quantity of ingredients
Rice variety any 1/2 cup / 60g. (little)..metal
Water 3 cups / 300g. (yes) .... earth
Lemon peel 1 piece / 3g. (yes) .... fire
Water 1/2 cup / 0g. (yes) .... earth
Carrot 2 pieces / 180g. (little)... earth
Celery sticks 1/2 piece / 5g. (recommended) .... earth
Champignon 1/2 cup / 50g. (recommended)............................... earth
Cress 2 table spoons / 20g. (recommended) ....metal
Linseed oil 1 dash / 3g. (recommended)................................... earth

Cooking instructions:
Cook rice according to basic recipe with a piece of lemon peel.
Steam chopped carrots, celery and mushrooms until soft.
Then sprinkle with cress. Then add a dash of high quality cold oil.

9.30 Roasted millet with Celery sticks

Strengthens spleen and kidney, diuretic, brings the liver Qi in motion,
cools heat, moisturizes, relaxes, builds up Qi, spreads.
Cooking time approx. 30 min
Calories p. portion: 400
2 portions
Allergens: L

Quantity of ingredients
Millet 1 cup / 120g. (yes) .... earth
Water 1 1/2 cups / 240g. (yes).. earth
Celery sticks 2 rods / 50g. (recommended)............................... earth
Water 2 table spoons / 30g. (yes)... earth
Herbs various 1 table spoon / 10g. (recommended).......................... *
Salt 1 pinch / 1g. (recommended)..water
Sage 3-4 leaves / 2g. (recommended)... fire
Cress 1 teaspoon / 3g. (recommended)....................................metal

Cooking instructions:
Roast millet briefly, pour over water, heat till it boils and let stand for 20 min. to swell.

Cut celery into small pieces and mix with water, salt and fresh herbs and cook for 10 min. Add to the millet. Sprinkle fresh sage or watercress over it.

9.31 Semolina slices

Nourishes fluids, moisturises dryness, produces humors, moisturizes intestines, cools inner heat, builds up Qi, spreads, moisturizes, preserves the fluids, contracts.
Cooking time approx. 30 min
Calories p. portion: 331
1 portions
Allergens: AG

Quantity of ingredients
Cow's milk (whole milk 3.5% fat) 3/4 cup - 6 oz / 200g. (yes) ....*
Wheat semolina 1 oz / 30g. (recommended)..............................wood
Butter organic 1 teaspoon / 3g. (yes)...earth
Banana 3 oz / 80g. (yes) ....earth
Orange juice 1 teaspoon / 3g. (yes)...wood

Cooking instructions:
Preheat the oven to 200°C/392°F (gas level 3). Heat 125 ml. of milk till it boils and let the semolina trickle in. Cook over medium heat. Stir in the butter. Spread the porridge in a ragout fin-frying pan, bake in the oven (center) in light brown for about 15 minutes. Puree the remaining milk with the banana and the orange juice and pour everything into a deep dish. Remove the porridge, cut into slices and place next to the sauce.

9.32 Tea from basil

Dries out, passes downwardly.
Cooking time approx. 10 min
Calories p. portion: 0
4 portions

Quantity of ingredients

Basil 1 teaspoon / 2g. (recommended) ....metal
Water 2 cup / 500g. (yes).. earth

Cooking instructions:

Heat the water till it boils and put it aside. Add basil and 10 min. to let go. Sweet to taste with honey.

9.33 Tea from celery sticks

Brings the Liver Qi in motion, cools heat, moisturizes, relaxes, builds up Qi, spreads.
Cooking time approx. 15 min
Calories p. portion: 1
4 portions
Allergens: L

Quantity of ingredients

Celery sticks 2 table spoons (chopped) / 18g. (recommended) .. earth
Water 2 cup / 500g. (yes).. earth

Cooking instructions:

Heat the water till it boils and put it aside. Add cutted celery and cook for 10 min. to let go. Strain. Sweet to taste with honey.

9.34 Tea from elderberry blossom tea

Derives wind-cold and wind-heat.
Cooking time approx. 10 min
Calories p. portion: 7
4 portions

Quantity of ingredients

Elderberry blossom tee 4 teaspoons / 12g. (yes).......................... fire
Water 2 cup / 500g. (yes).. earth

Cooking instructions:

Heat the water till it boils and put it aside. Add elderberry blossom tea and 10 min. to let go. Sweet to taste with honey. Strain when pouring.

9.35 Tea from Melissa

Preserves the fluids, contracts, soothes liver fire, stimulates lungs Qi.
Cooking time approx. 10 min
Calories p. portion: 0
4 portions

Quantity of ingredients
Balm 2 teaspoons / 4g. (recommended) .... wood
Water 2 cup / 500g. (yes) .... earth

Cooking instructions:
Heat the water till it boils and put it aside. Add lemon balm and 10 min.
to let go. Sweet to taste with honey. Strain when pouring.

9.36 Tea from peppermint with white sugar

Cools heat, distributes mucus, derives wind-cold and wind-heat, brings
the stomach Qi in motion, solves congestion, forces Qi, moisturizes
lungs.
Cooking time approx. 15 min
Calories p. portion: 8
2 portions

Quantity of ingredients
Peppermint 1 table spoon / 7g. (recommended) .... metal
Water 2 cup / 500g. (yes) .... earth
Sugar candy white 1 teaspoon / 3g. (yes) .... earth

Cooking instructions:
Heat the water till it boils and put it aside. Add peppermint and 10 min.
to let go. Strain. Sweet to taste with honey.

9.37 Tea from seaweed

Forces heart and kidneys Yin.
Cooking time approx. 10 min
Calories p. portion: 0
4 portions

Quantity of ingredients
Hijiki 2 teaspoons / 2g. (recommended)..................................... water
Water hot 2 cup / 500g. (yes) .... *

Cooking instructions:
Simmer the Hijiki alga with hot water for about 10 minutes. Then drink broth.

9.38 Tsampa with jam or fruit compote

Nourishes fluids, reduces stomach heat, forces spleen, produces essence, harmonizes stomach, moisturizes intestines.
Cooking time approx. 5 min
Calories p. portion: 280
1 portions
Allergens: AGO

Quantity of ingredients

Tsampa 2 table spoons / 30g. (recommended).......................... earth
Water 6-8 table spoons / 70g. (yes)... earth
Butter organic 1/2 teaspoon / 2g. (yes)..................................... earth
Strawberry jam 1 table spoon / 7g. (recommended)................... wood
Sunflower seeds 2 teaspoons / 14g. (yes) .... earth
Apple (sweet) 1 piece grated / 120g. (yes)................................ earth

Cooking instructions:

Pour tsampa with boiling water and stir with a spoon until a porridge is formed.
Add butter, jam, sunflower seeds and grated apple.
Sweet to taste with honey, whole cane sugar, or barley malt.
Spices and herbs: fresh mint, vanilla or cocoa, anise, cinnamon

Summer: jam or compote of your choice
Winter: nuts and apple or pear

9.39 Wheat fresh grain porridge with pears.

Moisturizes lungs, cools heat, reduces lung mucus, nourishes Yin from heart and kidney, forces heart and kidney, moisturizes, relaxes, builds up Qi, spreads.
Cooking time approx. 25 min
Calories p. portion: 309
2 portions
Allergens: ANO

Quantity of ingredients

Wheat 1 cup / 100g. (recommended)...wood
Water 2-4 cups / 350g. (yes) .... earth
Pear 2 pieces / 300g. (recommended)...................................... earth
Raisins 1 table spoon / 10g. (little).. earth
Sesame, white 1 table spoon / 8g. (yes).................................. earth
Sunflower seeds 1 table spoon / 8g. (yes) .... earth
Cardamom 1 pinch / 0,3g. (recommended).......................................*
Salt 1 pinch / 0,3g. (recommended)...water

Cooking instructions:

Preparation the night before: Wheat roughly cut; soak overnight.

In the morning: Put the wheat meal with a little hot water; simmer with stirring for about 15 minutes.
Meanwhile, add pear compote, raisins, crushed sesame, sunflower seeds, some ground cardamom, a small pinch of salt.

Variants: with grated apple or seasonal fruit.

10 Effects of food

10.1 Use ingredients: recommendable

Acai powder
Acerola fruit nectar or powder
Agar agar (kelp)
Agave nectar
Agrimony
Almond
Amaranth Pops
Angelica root
Apple juice (natural cloudy)
Apple puree
Apricot dried
Apricot jam
Apricot nectar
Apricots juice
Avocado
Baking powder
Balm
Banchatee (green tea)
barberry
Barley
Barley flour
Barley grass powder
Barley grouts
Barley malt
Barley not peeled
Basic recipe for a beef soup
Basic recipe for a beef soup (warming)
Basic recipe for a chicken soup
(warming)
Basic recipe for a fish soup
Basic recipe for a rice soup (Congee)
Basic recipe for a vegetable soup
(nutritious)
Basil
Basil (fresh)
Batavia
Bay leaf
Beans (green, fresh)
Bearberry leaf
Beef heart (calf)
Beef Oxtail pieces
Beef soup meat
Beer (alcohol-free)
Beer (alcohol-reduced)
Berries of the season
Berry juice
Bitter Herb liqueur
Bitter Lemon
Bitter liqueur

Bitter orange peel
Black beans
Black caraway
Black fungus mushroom
Blackberry dried (unripe fruit)
Blackberry jam
Blackberry leaves
Blackthorn (Sloe)
Blue mallow tee
Blueberry dried
Blueberry jam
Bocksdorn fruits (Fructus Lycii, Goji,
goji berry dried
Borage oil
Brazil nuts
Bread roll
Bread with carob kernel flour
Breadcrumbs (wheat bread, bread roll)
Brie cheese
Brown ale
Buckbean
Buckwheat
Buckwheat whole grain
Bush beans
Butter (half fat)
Butter beans white
Calamari
Camembert
Campari
Cantaloupe
Capers in olive oil
Cardamom
Carob flour, St. john's bread
Celery sticks
Chamomile
Chamomile tea
Champignon
Channa-Dal
Chenpi (chinese tangerine bowl)
Cherry (sour)
Cherry compote
Chervil
Chervil dried
Chestnut puree
Chicken Blood
Chicken egg white
Chicken yolk
Chickweed
Chicory

Chinese pearl barley
Chocolate (Diabetic)
Chrysanthemum blossom tea
Clarified butter
Clementine
Coconut fat
Coconut meat
Codfish
Cola drink
Cola drink (low calorie)
Compote (fruits of the season)
Cooking oil
Coriander (fresh)
Corn (fast polenta)
Corn (roasted)
Corn flour
Corn germ oil
Corn silk tea
Corn starch
Cottage cheese
Cranberries
Cranberry
Cranberry jam
Cream (30% fat)
Cream 10% coffee cream
Cream sour 10%
Cream sour 20%
Cream sour 30%
Creamer
Créme fraiche cheese
Cress
Crispbread
Crucian
Cucumber
Cucumber (bitter)
Cucumber (spicy cucumber)
Currant jam (black)
Currant jam (red)
Currant juice (black)
Currants (black)
Currants (red)
Curry paste red
Daisy
Dandelion (young plants)
Dashi
Dates red
Deer's Bones
Deer's kidneys
Duck (slaughtered)
Ducks egg
Dulse (seaweed)
Dyer's broom herb
Edam cheese
Eel smoked

Elderberries
Emmental cheese
Endive salad
Evening primrose oil
Fennel
Fennel seeds ground
Fenugreek (Trigonella foenum-graecum)
Fernet Branca (herbal bitter liqueur)
Feta cheese
Fish innards
Fish remains
Fish sauce
Flounder
Flower pollen
Fox nut, gorgon nut, makhana
Fresh cheese
Fresh cheese from soya
Fresh cheese with herbs
Freshwater crab
Fructose (glucose)
Fruit mix juice
Fruit tea
Gail plum
Galangal
Garam Masala powder
Gelatin white
Gelee Royal
Gentian root
Gentian root tea
Ginger oil
Ginkgo fruit
Ginseng
Ginseng liqueur
Ginseng root
Goat and sheep's blood
Goat and sheep's brain
Goat and sheep's liver
Goat and sheep's stomach
Goose blood
Goose fat
Gorgonzola
Gouda cheese
Grapefruit dried peel
Grapeseed oil
Greengage
Ground
Ground caraway
Guava
Halibut (Flatfish)
Hawthorn
Herbal tea mix
Herbs bitter
Herbs of Provence

Herbs various
Herbs wild
Hibiscus
Hibiscus tea
Hijiki
Hokkaido pumpkin
Honey wine (Met)
Hop
Horehound leaves
Horse meat
Jasmine blossoms tee
Jellyfish
Kaki plum
Kalmus
King Solomon's-seal
Kombu seaweed (Saccharina japonica)
Kudzu
Kukicha tea
Ladyfingers
Lamb kidneys
Lamb liver
Lamb's lettuce
Lavender blossoms
Leaf salads (bitter)
Lemon
Lemon Balm (dried)
Lemon Balm (fresh)
Lemongrass
Lettuce
Licorice root tea
Lily bulbs
Lima beans
Lime blossom tea
Linseed
Linseed (crushed)
Linseed oil
Liver smoothing tea
Loquate / Japanese medlar
Lotus roots
Lotus seeds
Lovage seeds
Luo Han Guo fruit
Lychee liqueur
Lye roll
Mallow (Malva sylvestris) blossom tea
Mango juice
Manioc flour
Mare's milk
Martini
Mascarpone cheese
Mayonnaise 50%
Mayonnaise 80%
Medlar
Mineral water

Mirabelle plum
Miso
Miso black (fermented)
Mixed Pickles
Mu Erh Mushroom
Muesli
Mulled Wine Spice
Multi-grain bread (gray bread)
Mung bean
Mustard
Mustard Dijon
Mustard medium hot
Mustard sweet
Nasturtium (nose-twister or nose-tweaker)
Nectarine
Nettles
Noodles (wheat) with egg
Noodles (wheat, lasagne) with egg
Noodles (wheat, ribbon noodles) with egg
Noodles (wheat, spaghetti) with egg
Noodles (whole grain) with egg
Nori, purple seaweed, red algae
Oat milk
Octopus
Olive oil
Olives green
Orange blossom
Orange dried peel
Orange grated peel
Orange jam
Orange peel
Oregano dried
Oregano fresh
Oyster shell powder
Oysters
Palm oil
Parsley root
Passion blossoms tea
Passion fruit
Peanut (roasted)
Peanut butter
Pear
Pearl barley
Pearl barley
Pepper powder (hot)
Peppermint
Peppermint tea
Pepperoni
Pepperoni, red, pitted, halved
Pepperoni, yellow, pitted, halved
Peppers (sweet)
Peppers powder

Pickle
Pig blood
Pigeon egg
Pinto beans speckled
Plum dried
Plums
Pork Bacon
Pork brain
Pork fat (lard)
Pork ham
Pork ham cooked
Pork ham smoked
Pork kidneys
Pork Lard
Pork lung
Pork marrow bones
Pork sausage (Bratwurst) Pork/beef sausage (smoked)
Pork's intestine
Potato (mealy)
Potato flour
Prickly pear
Processed cheese 12%
processed cheese 30%
Prosecco
Psyllium seed
Pudding powder vanilla
Puff pastry
Pumpernickel (dark bread)
Rabbit (wild)
Radicchio
Radish horseradish
Radish leaves
Raspberry jam
Raspberry leaf tea
Red beet
Red berry (without sugar)
Reishi mushroom
Ribworttea
Rice (fragrance)
Rice (Gaoliang / Sorghum)
Rice Basmati
Rice mash
Rice starch
Rice sticky
Rose blossom tea
Rose hip
Rose leaf tea
Rosefish
Rucola
Rum
Rusk
Rye wholemeal bread
Safflower (Dyer's thistle / Hong Hua)

Sage
Salt
Salt (herbal)
Savory
Savoy cabbage / kale
Sea buckthorn
Sea cucumber
Sesame oil roasted
Sesame, black
Sheep's milk
Sheep's milk yoghurt
Sherry (whine)
Shrimps
Skim milk powder
Slug
Sourdough
Soy flour
Soy noodles
Soy Tofu smoked
Soya Cuisine (soy cream)
Soybeans
Soybeans, blacks, fermented
Spelled flakes
Spirit
Spurdog (spiny dogfish, Schillerlocken)
St. Benedict's thistle, blessed thistle, holy thistle, spotted thistle
Stevia (candyleaf, sweetleaf)
Strawberry jam
Sugar - icing sugar
Sugar molasses
Sugar palm sugar
Sugar substitute (sweetener)
Supplementary nutrition
Tabasco
Tea mixture uric acid lowering
Thistle oil
Thyme dried
Toast bread (whole grain)
Tomato
Tomato dried
Tomato juice
Tomato paste
Tomato puree
Tonic Water
Trout (smoked)
Truffle
Tsampa (roasted barley flour)
Turkey ham
Turmeric (yellow root)
Turnip
Turnips
Umeboshi paste
Valerian

Vanilla pod
Vanilla sugar natural
Vinegar (Red wine vinegar)
Vinegar Aceto Balsamico
Vinegar Aceto Balsamico white
Wakame
Walnut oil
Walnuts roasted
Watermelon
Wax gourd
Wheat
Wheat flakes
Wheat flatbread/pita bread
Wheat flour whole grain
Wheat germ oil
Wheat semolina
Wheat semolina for children
Wheat/Rye/Gray-black bread with yeast
Wheatgrass juice
Wheatgrass powder
Whey
White bread (baguette)

White bread (pretzel sticks)
White bread (roll)
White bread (wheat bread)
White breadcrumbs
White cabbage
White dumpling bread (wheat bread cut into chunks)
Whitefish
Whole grain bread
Wholemeal flour
Wild garlic (garlic spinach)
Wild herbs
Wild strawberries
Wormwood
Wormwood herb
Yam root, yam root tuber
Yarrow
Yeast
Yew nut
Yoghurt vanilla
Yogurt (natural, 1.5% fat)
Yogurt (natural, 3.5% fat)

10.2 Use ingredients: yes

Adzuki beans
Amaranth
Apple (sour)
Apple (sweet)
Arrowroot
Artichoke
Asparagus (green or white)
Aubergine
Bamboo shoots
Banana
Banana (cooking banana)
Basic recipe for a duck soup
Beer (Pils)
Beer (Top-fermented German dark beer)
Blackberry´s
Black-eyed peas
Blueberry
Blueberry juice
Boletus mushroom
Borage
Broad beans (thick beans)
Broccoli
Brussels sprouts
Bulgur (cereals)
Burdock root tea
Butter organic
Buttermilk
Carambola (Star fruit)

Carp
Cashews
Cauliflower
Caviar
Celery root
Chanterelle
Chard
Chicken egg
Chickpeas
Chinese cabbage
Chlorella (fresh water)
Clementines
Coconut flakes
Coconut grated
Coix (seeds) YiYi Ren
Corn
Couscous
Cow's milk (1.5% fat)
Cow's milk (whole milk 3.5% fat)
Crab
Cranberry
Cranberry juice
Cream, sweet 30%
Curd cheese 20%
Curd cheese 40%
Currant (black)
Currant (red)
Currant (white)
Dandelion juice

Dandelionroots tea
Duck (heart)
Elderberry blossom tee
Fig
Fig dried
Fish pieces mixed (fresh water)
Freshwater fish
Gooseberry
Gourd
Grape juice red
Grape juice white
Grapefruit (Pomelo)
Grapefruit juice
Grapes red
Grapes white
Hazelnuts
Honey
Iceberg lettuce
Kefir
Kidney beans (red)
Kiwi
Lamb's lettuce
Lemon juice
Lemon peel
Lentils
Lentils black
Lentils red
Lentils yellow
Lime
Lychee
Lychee in Preserved
Malt
Mango
Maple syrup
Margarine
Margarine (diet)
Millet
Millet flakes
Miso paste (soy bean paste)
Morel (black, dried)
Morel, dried
Mozzarella
Mulberry fruit
Mullet
Mung bean sprouting
Mussels
Octopus
Olives
Orange
Orange juice
Parmesan
Parsnip
Peanut oil
Peanuts

Pear juice
Peas
Peas, green
Pigeon
Pine nuts
Pineapple
Pineapple juice without sugar
Pistachios
Plum
Potato
Pumpkin seeds
Quail
Quail egg
Quince
Quinoa
Radish black
Rapeseed oil
Raspberry
Raspberry dried (immature)
Red cabbage
Rhubarb
Rice long grain rice
Rice noodles
Romaine lettuce / lettuce salad
Rye
Rye flour
Saffron
Salmon
Salsify
Sauerkraut (cutted cabbage fermented)
Seacrab
Sesame oil
Sesame paste (Tahini)
Sesame, white
Shiitake, dried
Sorrel
Sour cherries
Sour cream 15% fat
Sour milk
Soy sauce
Soy Tofu
Soybean milk
Soybeans, black
Soybeans, yellow
Spelled (Dark) bread
Spelled grain
Spelled semolina
Spelled wholemeal flour
Spinach
Strawberries
Strawberry Juice
Sugar candy white
Sugar cane sugar
Sugar fructose - fruit sugar

Sugar glucose - grapes sugar
Sugar Milk Sugar
Sugar white
Sunflower oil
Sunflower seeds
Sweet potato
Tangerine
Tarragon (Estragon)
Topinambur
Trout
Vanilla

Vanilla powder
Vegetable juice
Water
Water hot
Wheat beer
Wheat bran
Wheat bulgur
Wheat flour
White beans
Yarrow tea
Zucchini

10.3 Use ingredients: little

Almond marzipan
Almond milk
Almond puree
Aloe juice
Apricot
Apricots
Boxhorn clover seeds
Carrot
Carrot (Early Carrot)
Carrot juice without sugar
Cereal coffee
Chestnuts
Coconut milk
Corn Grease (Polenta)
Curcuma
Dates dried
Feta cheese
French beans
Grass carp
Hyssop
Juniper berry
Lamb bones
Lamb meat
Lamb shoulder
Longane
Oat flour
Oat meal

Okra
Oyster mushroom
Papaya
Parsley
Peppers
Peppers (rose peppers)
Pineapple (from a can)
Poppy
Pumpkin
Pumpkin seed oil
Raisins
Rice (whole grain)
Rice black
Rice flour
Rice malt
Rice red
Rice round grain
Rice sweet
Rice variety any
Rice wild (nature rice)
Rosemary
Sago (cereals)
Soybean oil
Sugar brown
Thyme
Walnuts

10.4 Do not use contra-acting foods

Anchovy / Sardine
Anise (Common Fennel)
Bean oil
Beef bone marrow
Beef fillet
Beef heart
Beef kidney
Beef liver
Beef lungs (calf)

Beef meat
Beef meat (calf)
Beef meatbones
Beef stomach
Black tea
Buckwheat (roasted) Kasha
Cherry
Cherry juice
Chicken heart

Chicken liver
Chicken meat
Chicken stomach
Chili (pod or ground)
Chives
Chocolate
Cinnamon ground
Cinnamon sticks
Clove
Cocoa
Cod
Coffee
Coriander
Cumin (Caraway seed)
Curry
Deer meat
Deer meat
Dill
Eel
Fennel tea
Garlic
Ginger fresh
Ginger powder
Goat
Goat and sheep's milk
Goat cheese
Goose
Goose egg
Goose parts
Green spelt
Green tea
Herring
Kohlrabi
Kumquats
Leek
Lobster
Lovage
Mackerel
Marjoram
Mediterranean fish (cod, plaice,
haddock, sea Mold cheese
Mustard seeds
Mutton
Mutton
Nutmeg

Oat
Oat flakes (whole grain)
Oat flakes roasted
Oat fusion (baby food)
Onion (shallot)
Onion (spring onion)
Onion read
Onion white
Peaches
Peaches (canned)
Pepper (ground)
Pepper Cayenne
Pepper white (ground)
Peppercorns
Perch
Pheasant
Pimento
Plaice
Pomegranate
Pork heart
Pork knuckle
Pork liver
Pork meat
Pork skin
Pork stomach
Rabbit
Rabbit liver
Rabbit meat
Radish
Radish (white, green, purple-red)
Red wine
Rose hip tea
Sake
Shark
Shrimp
Sour milk cheese 20%
Spiny lobsters
Star anise
Tuna
Turkey breast meat
Umebcshi plums (Japanese apricots)
Vinegar (Apple vinegar)
White wine
Wild boar meat
Yogi tea

11 Herbs and their effects

11.1 Basil

thermal effect: warm
taste: spicy, bitter
Dries out, leads down. Tonifies Yang and Qi, dissolves mucus-cold, eliminates wind-cold.
It has a beneficial effect on flatulence and nausea, relaxing and soothing.
Good to fight emphysema, bronchitis, whooping cough, high blood pressure, headache, mouth odor, warts, hiccup, gout, migraine.

11.2 Herbs various

thermal effect: taste:
Stimulates appetite. Effect different.
Appetizing, lots of trace elements and vitamins.

11.3 Cress

thermal effect: cool
taste: sweet
Moves and tonifies qi and blood, diuretic, cools in internal heat, moisturizes lungs, triggers stagnation, heads upwards.
Diuretic, supports urination. Good to fight dry mouth, inner agitation, sore throat, diabetes, kidney stones, gastrointestinal complaints, lung problems, menstrual cramps or cancer.

11.4 Lovage

thermal effect: warm
taste: spicy, bitter
Reduces inner wind and moisture, dissolves stagnation, directs upward, warms Yang, regulates and moves Qi, warms inside, dissolves mucus-cold, eliminates wind-cold.
Stimulates digestion, reduces pain. Extracts of the root are used to flush out urinary tract infections and prevent kidney gravel.

11.5 Lily bulbs

thermal effect: cool
taste: sweet, bitter
Tonifies Yin, soothes Shen / Spirit. Moisturizes the lungs, clears heat and stops coughing.

Calms nerves, good to fight scaly skin. The onions and the petals are added to ointments in the Orient, which can heal muscles and tendons. White lily (astringent).

11.6 Balm

thermal effect: warm
taste: bitter
Keep the fluids, pulls together, soothe lever fire, soothe Shen, stimulate Lung Qi. Regulates qi, eliminates heat caused by yin deficiency.
Soothing effect, Good for insomnia, restlessness and upset stomach, Allergies, Asthma, Migraine, Flatulence, Headache, Rheumatism and mental tension. To strengthen after cold and infectious diseases.

11.7 Parsley

thermal effect: warm
taste: bitter
Nourishes blood and liver, harmonizes liver and spleen, strengthens eyesight, preserves juices, contracts. Dissolves moisture and warms Yang.
Stimulates liver function, detoxifies. Forces urinating. Relieves flatulence. Digestive and menstrual stimulating, birth-accelerating, memory-enhancing, blood-purifying, skin-smoothing.

11.8 Peppermint

thermal effect: cool
taste: spicy, bitter
Cools heat, expels mucus, dissipates wind-cold and wind-heat, moves stomach qi, releases congestion, tonifies, regulates and moves qi.
Relaxes, frees the lungs and the nose (inhale), regulates the cycle.
Stimulates bile flow and bile production, antispasmodic in gastrointestinal disorders, antimicrobial and antiviral.

11.9 Sage

thermal effect: neutral
taste: bitter, spicy
Expels slime, guides down, strengthens Qi, eliminates Wind-Heat, eliminate heat induced by Yin deficiency.
Good to fight yeast infections. The leaves have a digestive effect and are used in greasy foods. Antiperspirant effect. Helps to relieve coughing attacks. Dries out.

11.10 King Solomon's-seal

thermal effect: neutral
taste: sweet, bitter
Tonifies Yin and Qi, astringent, tonifies blood, eliminates wind-cold / heat-wetness.
Used to repair wounds or damaged tissue. Good to fight dry cough, earlier also tuberculosis and dysentery, as well as diarrhea and hemorrhoids.

11.11 Yam root, yam root tuber

thermal effect: neutral
taste: sweet
Tonifies Yin, Yang and Qi, reduces inner wind, dissolves wetness, warms Yang.
Solves cramps (in the gastrointestinal tract). Digestive through increased bile production. Anti-inflammatory in rheumatic diseases.
Mucolytic agent for coughing. Relief of menopausal symptoms.

12 Basics of Nutrition

The basic principles of nutrition described herein are general recommendations. They are not aimed at a specific form of therapy. Recommendations concerning a therapy have priority.

12.1 Nutrition

Regular meals in a relaxed atmosphere. A warm breakfast is considered a good start into the day.
The main meals ought to be taken for lunch – supper in the early evening. Pay attention to feeling hungry or sated: don't eat too much nor remain hungry is the rule
Prepare the meals freshly from natural, regional products. Frozen, heat-conserved, industrially prepared or foodstuffs cooked in the microwave oven are rejected.
Choice of foodstuffs according to the season: more cooling food in summer, more warming food in winter.
Eat cooked food at least twice a day. Food and drinks ought to be lukewarm, never ice-cold or hot.
Raw vegetables, briefly cooked vegetables, freshly squeezed juices and mineral water are not recommended. Milk and dairy products are only included in the diet if they don't cause problems. Don't use therapeutic recipes over a longer period without consulting your doctor or therapist.

Varied food
Enjoy the diversity of foodstuffs. Characteristics of a balanced nutrition are variety, suitable combination and a balanced quantity of rich and low energy foodstuffs (on one hand avoiding undersupply with essential nutrients and on the other hand to take to many undesirable substances).

A lot of Cereal Products - and Potatoes
Bread, pasta, rice, cereal flakes (best wholemeal) as well as potatoes contain almost no fat, but many vitamins, mineral nutrients, trace elements, roughage and secondary plant substances. These foodstuffs ought to be taken with low-fat side dishes.

Vegetables and Fruit – „Take Five" every day ... 5 portions of
vegetables and fruit a day, as fresh as possible, briefly cooked, or maybe one portion as a juice – ideal as a side dish to every meal as well as snack between meals: Thus a lot of vitamins, mineral nutrients as well as roughage and secondary plant substances

Daily milk and dairy products

Milk and Dairy Products every Day, once or twice per Week Fish; meat, sausages as well as eggs moderately. These foodstuffs contain valuable nutrients like calcium in the milk, iodine selenium and omega-3 fat acids in saltwater fish. Meat is favorable due to its high content of disposable iron and the vitamins B1, B6 and B12. Quantities of 300 – 600 g meat and sausage per week are sufficient. Prefer low-fat products, especially in meat- and dairy products.

Low-fat and fatty Foodstuffs
Fat supplies us with essential fat acids and fatty foodstuffs contain also fat-soluble vitamins. Fat is high in energy; therefore much fat in the food may cause overweight, possibly also cancer. Too many saturated fat acids may further a tendency for cardio-vascular diseases in the long term. Prefer vegetable oils and fats (e.g. rapeseed-, olive-, soya-oils and solid fats produced therefrom). Beware of invisible fat in meat- and dairy products, pastry and sweets as well as in fast-food and convenience foods. 70 – 90 g fat per day is sufficient.

Moderately Sugar and Salt
Take sugar and foods/drinks containing various kinds of sugar (e.g. glucose syrup) only occasionally. Use herbs and spices as well as a little salt creatively. Prefer salt containing iodine.

Plenty of Liquids
Water is absolutely essential. Drink 1-2 l liquids every day. Prefer water (with or without gas) and other low-calorie drinks. Alcoholic drinks should not be taken.

Tasty Dishes, carefully cooked
Cook the meals with as low temperatures and as short as possible, using little water and fat – this preserves the original taste, keeps the nutrients intact and prevents the production of harmful compounds.

Take time and enjoy the food
Take your Time and enjoy your Food
Eating consciously helps to eat right. The eye enjoys food, too. It's fun, invites to enjoy varied dishes and stimulates the feeling of satiety.

Watch your Weight and stay in Motion
A balanced diet and a lot of exercise and sport (30 – 60 min/day) are a healthy combination. The right weight furthers well-being and health.
Thermals, directional effectiveness, digestive power
There are various criteria for judging the effectiveness of herbs and

foodstuffs.

The use of certain herbs and ingredients is based on observations of the effects on the body which these foodstuffs, herbs and spices show after having eaten them. The medical science has developed following system: Every ingredient or herb has a directional effectiveness. Furthermore, there are herbs which have a special effect or certain organs.

The basic condition for a healthy metabolism is to obtain sufficient energy from food and that the digestive process doesn't use too much energy. An easily digestible meal makes content and sated, doesn't cause flatulence and fatigue after the meal. The perfect spices increase the healthiness of our meals. Very often, just small doses of herbs and spices will suffice. They are not used to make us sated, but to help our digestive organs to digest the food.

12.2 Recipes

The recipes list the ingredients to be used and the cooking instructions show how the dish is prepared. The list of ingredients shows the concerned quantities as well as the relevance for the therapy. If you find „less than mentioned", try to comply or find an alternative from the „list of recommended foodstuffs". Mostly it shall result just in a small change of taste when you simply avoid this ingredient.

Mild cooking methods: boiling, stewing poaching, steaming
Strong cooking methods: barbecuing, roasting, frying, smoking
Balanced cooking methods: deep-frying, baking brick
Deep-freezing and warming in the microwave oven should be avoided (denaturalization).

12.3 Foodstuffs

Foodstuffs have an effect on body and soul like medicinal herbs, only a very much milder one. Dietary advice is mainly based on regional foodstuffs. The knowledge about the effects of each foodstuff and the knowledge, when which foodstuff shall be used, is based on the orthodox school of medicine. Use ecologic-organic products, if possible. As everything should be cooked for a long time due to a better digestability and very rarely eaten raw, the food agrees with everyone.

The classification of the foodstuffs according to their effect on the body is the basis in order to achieve a harmon ous status of health.

Dietary advisors do not recommend certain foodstuffs for everyone. The individual diet is tailor-made for the individual constitution.

Buy only fresh and ripe fruit and vegetables. You ought to leave unripe fruit and vegetables and such with brown spots and wilted leaves behind in the market. In this case take deep-frozen goods (never ready-to-serve dishes!). Fruit and vegetables are deep-frozen immediately after harvesting and often contain more vitamins and minerals than the goods from the vegetable shelf. Whereas conserved or tinned goods contain very much less biological substances. Also, salt, sugar and others are mostly added to the latter. Never leave the foodstuffs in the water after washing them to avoid that many vital substances get drowned. Clean salads, fruit and vegetables immediately before serving.

Please make sure of the hygienic processing of foodstuffs. Clean your salads, fruit and vegetables carefully. When cooking with meat, prepare all ingredients first and then process the meat products. Clean the worktop and tools very carefully. Wooden surfaces ought to be treated with a mild disinfectant regularly in order to reduce germination. Store fruit and vegetables separately, if possible. Harvested fruit and vegetables are still alive and emit e.g. ethylene gas, which makes other products ripen and age faster. Keep meat and fish in the closed packaging or store them in the fridge in closed containers.

12.4 Herbs

There are some basic rules for storing medicinal herbs. On principle, herbs must be protected from direct sunlight, humidity and heat.

Containers for the storage of herbs may be glasses, ceramic jars and even plastic containers. However, plastic is a rather unsuitable material and should only be a short-term solution. In case of glass containers, use a dark material.

Medicinal herbs cannot be kept for any long period. The shelf life of herbs is limited. However, it can be prolonged with suitable storage. The place should be dark, rather cool and absolutely dry. A wooden medicine cabinet, placed not directly next to a source of heat, would be ideal. Never buy large quantities of herbs so as not to have to throw them away. Label the container with the name of the herb and the date of harvesting or processing.

13 Other dietic-books

The following syndromes of dietetics, TCM or for a therapy supplement for cancer are available.

Dietetics

E001. Nutrition of the infant - baby food
E002. Nutrition during lactation
E003. Nutrition in old age
E004. Nutrition of children and adolescents
E005. Nutrition of athletes
E006. Light weight
E007. Pregnancy
E008. Full food

Protein and electrolyte - kidneys
E009. (hemodialysis) dialysis treatment
E010. Acute renal failure
E011. Chronic renal insufficiency
E012. Nephrotic syndrome
E013. Kidney stones (nephrolithiasis)

Gastrointestinal tract - pancreas
E014. Acute pancreatitis (inflammation of the pancreas)
E015. Chronic pancreatitis (inflammation of the pancreas)

Gastrointestinal tract - small intestine and large intestine
E016. Acute obstipation (constipation)
E017. Chronic obstipation (constipation)
E018. Colon irritabile
E019. Diverticulitis
E020. Acquired lactose intolerance (lactose malabsorption)
E021. Fructose malabsorption
E022. Glutensensitive enteropathy (celiac disease)
E023. Colectomy
E024. Short Bowel Syndrome

Gastrointestinal tract - liver, gallbladder, bile ducts
E025. Acute and chronic hepatitis (inflammation of the liver)
E026. Cholelithiasis (bile stones)
E027. fatty liver
E028. cirrhosis

Gastrointestinal tract - Stomach and duodenal intestine
E029. Acute gastritis
E030. Chronic gastritis
E031. Stomach bleeding
E032. Ulcus ventriculi and duodenal ulcer
E033. Condition after gastric surgery

Gastrointestinal tract - oral cavity and esophagus
E034. Stomatitis
E035. Esophageal carcinoma (esophageal cancer)
E036. Refluosophagitis (heartburn)

Special diseases
E037. Phenylketonuria (PKU)
E038. Rheumatic joint diseases

Metabolism
E039. Obesity (overweight)
E040. Diabetes mellitus
E041. Eating disorders (underweight)

Fat metabolism
E042. Hypercholesterolaemia (increased cholesterol level)
E043. Hepatic Encephalopathy

Heart and circulation
E044. Arteriosclerosis (arterial calcification)
E045. Heart insufficiency
E046. Hypertension
E047. Hyperuricaemia and gout

Changed nutrient requirements
E048. In case of fever
E049. For malignant diseases
E050. After burns
E051. Radiation and chemotherapy

CANCER
E100. Pancreatic cancer
E101. Bladder cancer
E102. Blood cancer (leukemia)
E103. Breast cancer
E104. Colorectal cancer
E105. Gastric cancer
E106. Kidney cancer
E107. Esophageal cancer

TCM
E200. Bladder - moisture heat in the bladder
E201. Bladder - moisture and cold in the bladder
E202. Bladder - emptiness and cold in the bladder
E203. Large intestine - external cold affects the large intestine
E204. Large intestine - moisture heat in the large intestine
E205. Large intestine - heat blocks the intestine II acute
E206. Large intestine - dryness of the colon
E207. Large intestine - Yang deficiency (cold)
E208. Heart - Blood insufficiency
E209. Heart - Blood stagnation
E210. Heart - Fire
E211. Heart - Hot mucus clogs the heart pores

E212. Heart - Cold mucus clogs the heart pores
E213. Heart - Qi deficiency
E214. Heart - Yang deficiency
E215. Heart - Yin deficiency
E216. Liver - Ascending Liver Yang
E217. Liver - Blood deficiency
E218. Liver - Blood stagnation
E219. Liver - Moisture heat in liver and gall bladcer
E220. Liver - Fire
E221. Liver - Gall bladder Qi-Empty
E222. Liver - Cold in the liver meridian
E223. Liver - Qi stagnation
E224. Liver - Wind
E225. Liver - Wind with ascending liver Yang
E226. Liver - Wind with blood anemic
E227. Liver - Wind with extreme heat
E228. Lung - Qi deficiency
E229. Lung - Mucus-moisture in the lungs
E230. Lung - Mucus-heat in the lungs
E231. Lung - Mucus-cold in the lungs
E232. Lung - Dryness of the lungs
E233. Lung - Wind-heat attacks the lungs
E234. Lung - Wind-cold affects the lungs
E235. Lung - Yin deficiency
E236. Stomach - Bloodstagnation
E237. Stomach - Fire
E238. Stomach - Cold with liquid
E239. Stomach - Nutrition stagnation
E240. Stomach - Qi deficiency
E241. Stomach - Rebellious Qi
E242. Stomach - Yin Emptiness
E243. Spleen - Heat and moisture attack the spleen
E244. Spleen - Coldness and moisture affects the spleen
E245. Spleen - Qi deficiency
E246. Spleen - Qi deficiency + Declining spleen Qi
E247. Spleen - Qi deficiency + spleen does not control the blood
E248. Spleen - Yang deficiency
E249. Kidney - Heart and kidney no longer communicate
E250. Kidney - Jing deficiency
E251. Kidney - Kidneys cannot receive the Qi
E252. Kidney - Qi is not stable
E253. Kidney - Yang deficiency
E254. Kidney - Yin deficiency

For further information visit di-book.com.